FROM POVERTY & PRISON TO PURPOSE

A JOURNEY OF DISCOVERING FREEDOM

BY

DANIELLE C. GIDDINS

Danielle Cherise Giddins
www.daniellecgiddins.com

FORWARD

From Poverty and Prison to Purpose is Danielle Giddins's exploration of the journey she's taken from childhood to her rise as a successful entrepreneur, business coach and mentor, and a woman of faith and power.

Danielle shares the dark and challenging times she experienced on her journey. She writes personally and openly about the hardships she has faced, but also about how God has brought her out of the valley into His glorious light. Along the way, she also shares her struggles with learning how to overcome the lingering effects of childhood sexual abuse and the loss of a parent.

Throughout her book, Danielle uses her experiences to address the following themes:

- The pain of grief and loss
- Enduring through imprisonment
- Surviving abuse
- Embracing true beauty
- The role of faith in hope and healing

- Letting go of shame

- Overcoming lust and promiscuity

- Following your unique calling and passion

- Being a successful single parent

- Trusting God daily for hope and healing

In the darkness, Danielle knew God was there – but she wondered if she could trust Him. Even at her lowest point, when she saw no human way forward, God was at work, powerfully redeeming her story and calling her out of the dark.

Danielle tells her story with warmth and vulnerability, challenging us all to focus on God's purpose for our lives, surround ourselves with friends who will fight for us, and face life's challenges with courage and faith. If you've ever found yourself in a dark place as the result of grief, depression or loss, Danielle's story will reassure you that even when you're walking through dark valleys, God can and will lead you on a path to joy and hope.

It is a joy to pastor Danielle, and to witness firsthand her journey from "poverty and prison to purpose." Your life will be enriched as you read her story.

Lenyar Robinson, Pastor

I consider it an honor to introduce you to an amazing woman whom I call cousin, friend and sister. I'm her cheerleader and she's mine. She is an encourager and supporter to family, friends and others who God puts in her path. I've watched Danielle grow into an amazing woman who understands how to be in a relationship with Christ. Her faith has allowed her to overcome many obstacles in life and break generational curses. It was faith that allowed her to be vulnerable and follow the path to find her soulmate.

As you read her story, you'll see how God takes our imperfections and uses them to humble us and guide us into His purpose for our lives. You'll see yourself as Danielle shares her innermost thoughts, feelings and experiences. You'll laugh as she shares some of her craziest moments. You'll cry as she shares the griefs, pain and losses she experienced. By the end of the book, you'll see how life's struggles will make you stronger.

Danielle, thank you for having the courage to be authentically you. Here's to your continued elevation and success beyond your wildest dreams!

Kim "Kimbella" Campbell

I grew up with Danielle in a public housing project in Baltimore City called McCulloh Homes. We had a very close-knit community, where all the kids were raised as family. Danielle and I met at a very young age because our grandmothers and mothers were friends. We went to elementary and middle school together. As preteens we started meeting other people, but our friendship always remained strong.

Danielle and I went through so many things in several stages of our lives – different relationships, the births of our kids and the loss of our moms. This made our bond even stronger because we had to now face the realities of life. My friend went from being a teenage mom to having her second child at twenty-one and being imprisoned. This was extremely hard for me to watch. All I knew was that I had to step up and do what I was supposed to do as a friend and sister, and that was to be there and be of support. I remember being one of Danielle's three friends who visited, wrote letters and accepted collect phone calls.

This is all to say I watched my friend forgive, forget and evolve into the phenomenal woman and entrepreneur that she is today. In this book you will read about how Danielle didn't let the adversities and betrayal of others slow her down from rebirthing into Danielle Giddins.

    Takishia Harris

ACKNOWLEDGEMENTS

In loving memory of my mother, Sharon Marie Jackson. Thank you for giving me your absolute best. I have learned to appreciate the parts of me that were influenced by you over my journey to freedom, and for that I am forever grateful.

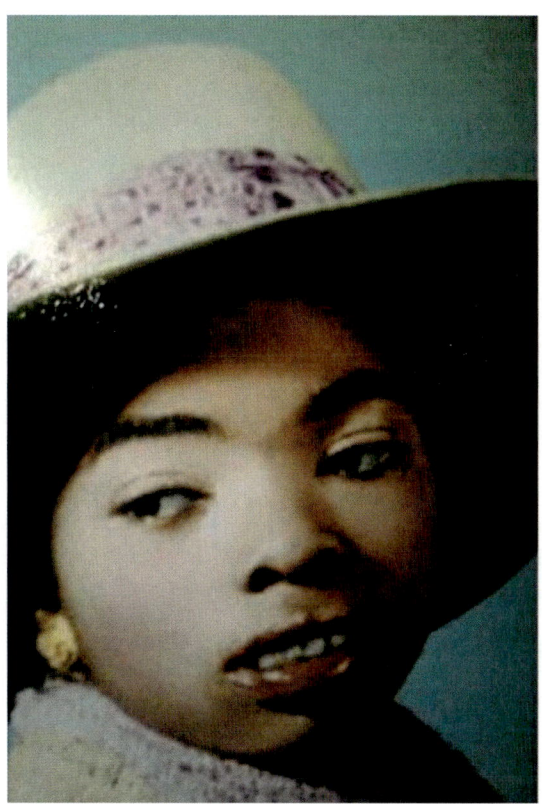

This book is dedicated to my daughters, Latia Cherise Milburn and Tykira Chanel Ceaser. Thank you for giving me a reason to  live and to fight to become greater than poverty. May the love I have for you translate into the legacy I continue to build so that you both become greater than me!

I want to first thank my human rock, my shero, my Olivia Pope and my angel, Cecelia M. Jackson, my grandmother. She was a hardworking woman prior to her retirement, a caring, kind and gracious professional who managed to support her children in the best way she knew how. She cared for my brother and me before and after my mother's death in every way she could, along with my daughters while I was creating a life for my own family. I love you, Grama. Thank you for being my guiding light on earth.

Thank you to my dearest friend Chelsea Scott and my cousin Kim Campbell, who love me unconditionally and authentically, chastise me, pray for me, encourage me and have been my biggest cheerleaders and positive influences in the last twenty years of my life during most of my internal growth. Thank you to my friend Yeve Montgomery for birthing the Writers Workshop project and coaching me during the foundation of writing this book. And thank you to my sister in love Ebony Vaughn for walking me through every process.

Thanks also to my spiritual leaders Apostle Kenneth Robinson and Pastor Lenyar Robinson, who have covered me, taught me, supported me, contributed to the knowledge and wisdom of my renewed mindset and offered me leadership training through the Dream Eagles Empowerment Network while displaying a wealth mindset for God's Kingdom. Your leadership and teaching evoked evolution in my spiritual, physical and financial life and in my business. I am living under the abundance of wealth transfer.

Last, my husband, Jamar John Giddins, who was the first to love me unconditionally as Christ loved the church and continues to fight to be the man God has called him to be for us. Thank you for loving me, supporting me and celebrating me, for allowing me to travel, the late-night pardons, the solo hotel lock-ins and the space to grow. Through every valley and mountain, I know you are still God's choice for me. The birth of this book is the end of an era for Danielle Rogers as I lay her to death – I leave this memoir as a testimony for God's healing and deliverance and as an example of becoming renewed in Christ as I fully embrace the new blood that has washed, cleansed and redeemed me as Danielle Giddins.

PREFACE

My daughters became the reason I saw a life worth living beyond the poverty I was born into, the pain that developed in me and not knowing my purpose for existing on this earth. So this book is for every young woman who has yet to discover her worth and purpose being made in the image of God.

In 2000, I was given my first journal by my career mentor to begin to release the anger, pain and destruction and the untold truth that lived inside of me. That one journal multiplied into twenty, and I kept them all to transfer to my daughters so they would know what I had gone through, hoping this would help them navigate life's trials. At the age of forty-three, I decided to create a library in my office of all the books I had accumulated, and I added my journals to the shelves. I began to read through the pages of my earlier years, and it was as if my oldest daughter were living the untold stories of my life. Fueled by so many emotions, but most of all failure as a mother because my daughter had repeated my mistakes, I decided against the transfer and destroyed them all. She would only have been looking in the mirror and knowing I had gone through the same thing instead of learning from my journey. In that moment I knew it was time for me to share the most intimate, vulnerable, shameful, embarrassing and unfiltered experiences of my life from the perspective of a mature, redeemed, virtuous woman, so that my daughters, young ladies, mothers and other women would be encouraged and would never give up on finding self-worth and their purpose in life, and so they would know that the love of God covers a multitude of our sins. **There is life after death!**

"No power in the sky above or in the earth below – indeed, nothing in all creation will ever be able to separate us from the love of God that is revealed in Christ Jesus our Lord" (Romans 8:39, NLT).

I wrote this book to speak to the young mothers who are raising their children swaddled in their pain, with little or no parental guidance beyond the walls of their poverty. For the mother who thinks teaching her children to "do as I say and not as they see" is effective, the contrary will be what drives their lives until they learn differently. To the woman who never knew or had a relationship with her father and is still learning how that has played a part in her behavior with men. To the woman who thinks the pain she feels is death and that there is no light – to her I say, truly, life after death exists in a relationship with God. To the man who does not realize that his internal issues with his mother and how she influenced him are directly reflected in his expectations in relationships with women. To the father who did not take dominion in his daughter's life to make his presence known and to build her up, to validate her worth, but instead left her, neglected, unprotected, unsure and unaware of the love of a father or a man. Whether the father was in the home, their encounters were limited or he was absent and she never knew him, it left her clueless in male interactive relationships. Thank you, Lord, for covering me.

In Psalm 27:10 (NKJV), the Word of God says, "When my mother and father forsake me, then the Lord will take care of me."

TABLE OF CONTENTS

FORWARD 3

ACKNOWLEDGEMENTS 9

PREFACE 13

BLOODLINES 17

501 HOFFMAN STREET 26

MY ADDICTION 36

A BROKEN PROMISE 48

IMPRISONMENT 56

FREEDOM AND LOSS 68

THE CROSSROADS 77

PARENTAL INFLUENCE 84

REDEMPTION 90

MY NAME CHANGE 102

THE CHOSEN GENERATION 114

BLOODLINES

It was a typical summer morning. We woke up, crust in our eyes and a stench on our breath. We put on our clothes from yesterday and sat on our front step – or maybe we walked to the store, or went to the playground, where other kids would join us. After a couple of hours, we would always go in, wash up, put on clean clothes and head back outside. That day, before going out, we made our way to the kitchen, where the light from the sun was shining on the clean countertop. At nightfall, darkness would bring out a flood of unwanted household guests by the hundreds – roaches. They would run rapidly to take cover back in their hidden places when the kitchen light was turned on, but just then, we were safe – the daylight would keep them away.

We saw peanut butter but no jelly and only two pieces of bread, including the end, so we each took one and removed the King syrup from the cabinet. We made our syrup sandwiches and left out the back door, only to be met by a loud shout – "HANDS UP AND DON'T MOVE!"

It was a police officer, pointing a gun in our faces. They had our house surrounded. Both my cousin Antwon and I began to cry. I couldn't tell you why he was crying, but for me it was the fact that we had dropped our syrup sandwiches on the ground and those were our last pieces of bread. Police visits and raids were a regular occurrence at our house because of the Jackson Five. Welcome to 501 West Hoffman Street, Baltimore, Maryland, 21201, the McCulloh Homes Projects, where I was born into sin and poverty on November 1st, 1973, Danielle Cherice Rogers, along with my twin, Darnell Maurice Rogers.

The McCulloh Homes Projects was one of the first public housing projects developed in the 1940s, exclusively for African Americans. It accommodated more people in a household than its predecessors, with four to five bedrooms, two baths and a front and back lawn – we had four bedrooms with a huge side yard on our end unit. It may sound like a new housing development from a well-known builder like Ryan Homes, but it was far from it. This development was impoverished, public housing for poor and low-income families.

When my grandmother Cecelia Jackson, known to most as Snooky but to me as Grama, was a child, she and her three siblings moved from place to place all the time. Once they settled in a new place only to move again after just three weeks. So she wanted to create stability for her children.

Grama worked part time at the Pink Pony Bar on the corner of North Avenue in Baltimore Maryland, to feed her children. My great-grandmother, Naomi Barnes, nicknamed Mama Sis, forced my grandmother to marry one Leroy Jackson at the age of nineteen and move out of the house. She already had her first daughter when they got married. Leroy was an alcoholic and physically and mentally abusive. One night she had enough abuse and called her brother, Ronald Mears and her uncles, who told her to pack the kids up, they were on the way. Leroy was beaten up pretty bad and told if he contacted her again he wouldn't see another day. (Abuse seems to run in our family – when Mama Sis sister, my Aunt Pauline, called a cab to pick her and her children up, she had lit the bed on fire while her husband was asleep after she'd endured a beating.) During the ten years prior to her escape, some nights my grandmother went to bed hungry because she only had enough food to portion out for the kids. She was living with her grandmother and working after life with Leroy. The oldest daughter, my Aunt Faye, watched the kids while she worked, and in 1973, Grama left her job at the bar and began her career with the government at Fort Meade Army base as a file clerk. As she increased her level of employment, she began to save money to move into her own place. She had a choice to remain with Grama Johnson or purchase a home, but she decided to jump on the new low-income townhome concept at McCulloh Homes Projects. She had conversations with a friend who was concerned about her moving to the projects because their reputation was bad, but my grandmother decided she would give it a try in 1971. The Jackson family moved, and for the next twenty-five years that was our family residence.

After the family had settled in, her youngest son, who was ten years old, said, "Mama, it's evil here, we have to move," and the whispers and discernment of a child turned out to be true. The McCulloh Homes Projects became the demise of the Jackson Five siblings, Larry, Ronald, Milton, Sharon and Warren. They had an older sister, Faye, who had a different dad and a different perspective growing up because she had to watch her siblings while my grandmother worked. Aunt Faye took a different path – she was the first and only child to complete school and go to Coppin State University to study criminal justice, and she landed a position in the Juvenile Public Defenders Office as a senior intake specialist, where she worked until her retirement in 2015 with thirty-four years of service. She got her own apartment in

Baltimore, but the generational curses showed themselves in her life also.

Grama climbed her way up the ladder at Fort Meade until she retired in 1996 as a GS11 who had supervised fifteen people in the Department of Army, Central Security, 902 Military Intelligence Group. She keeps in touch with all her team members, majors and colonels whom she interacted with and made an impact on over the years. I watched her work hard and earn respect within her career and as a supervisor. She was the only person from our house who got up and went to work consistently, and watching her keep a job and build lasting relationships gave me hope to become as successful when I became an adult.

Family was always the center point for us, and when we gathered, laughter always drowned any troubles of our hearts. I had an opportunity to meet my great-great-grandmother, Maude Virginia Davenport, who was a very light-skinned woman with long hair – she was part Indian mixed with her black. We called her Grama Johnson prior to her passing. Her mother was born a slave whose name was Hana Patton-Willis-Wallace-Fitzgerald-

Green-Henneson-Barrald. Why did she carry so many names? Because every slave owner attached their name when she was sold. She had been whipped so much that she developed large keloids on her back, which turned into a tumor that she never got removed. Maude married William Henry Johnson, who was white. He became a pastor and Grama Johnson gave birth to fifteen children. Two passed away during childbirth, and the family isn't sure what happened to two more, but I know of her seven boys and four girls, William, Jerome, Joseph, Randolph, Raymond, Samuel, Norman, Naomi, Blanche, Marjorie and Pauline Johnson. The Johnson boys were a little rough, often fighting, but nothing like the Jacksons. This was where our lineage met my life span, and that lineage came with its share of poverty, bondage and internal tribulation, which passed from the Johnsons to the Jacksons and branched out within our family tree.

Grama's mother, Naomi Barnes, nicknamed Mama Sis, was out exploring the world during the jazz era while other family members cared for her children. Mama Sis emotionally and physically abandoned her children, but from the day I can remember, she was present in my life. Her regrets about her abandonment were never talked about or spoken, but her actions revealed them. She was available in every way for her grandchildren and great-grandchildren, and that was her redemption for her past. Mama Sis was self-employed, working as a caregiver and home nurse for the matriarchs of Jewish families – I particularly remember the Kleins, Kaufmans and Zieglers. She was loyal to them and they loved her. When one matriarch passed away, she would be referred to another family. She went to their houses at seven p.m. and left at seven a.m., but she always stopped by 501 to check on us twins every morning prior to going home.

She made sure we ate, cleaned the kitchen, gave us baths in the sink with her uniform on. She would fuss and cuss if the house were out of tack and she would send the friends of my mother or uncles home from our couch. They were all fearful of Mama Sis. She was never sick and always said, "An aspirin a day will keep the doctor away," while never seeing a doctor until she fell and hit her head in a store at the age of seventy-six. Her favorite line was "I have all the family on my prayer list and pray for all by name individually every morning." When we got older, she introduced us to receiving an allowance for doing chores every Friday night. She would always show special attention to the grandchild or great-grandchild she felt needed the most attention or was in the most trouble. I would say my Uncle Warren and my mother got the most out of Mama Sis. She became their savior, advocate and bail out, and sometimes their enabler.

My grandmother, whose other relatives raised her while her mother was traveling and living life, never spoke her truth to Mama Sis and managed to raise all six of her children within the same household.

Genesis 50:24: "Soon I will die," Joseph told his brothers, "but God will surely come to help you and lead you out of this land of Egypt. He will bring you back to the land he solemnly promised to give to Abraham, to Isaac, and to Jacob."

501 HOFFMAN STREET

I was a born leader, preceding my twin brother by fifteen minutes into this world to do greater than what my mind, my family and others could imagine. I was the only girl of four grandchildren at the time. The odds were stacked against me and the more life happened the higher those stakes grew, but I can look back and see the hand of God protecting me always from physical harm or death.

Most of my immediate family resided at 501 Hoffman Street, with its four bedrooms. My mother, brother and I all slept in a queen-size bed in one room, along with my dad when I was young. My grandmother and her longtime boyfriend Andy, who later became her husband, slept in another room, and the four boys shared the other two rooms, when they weren't incarcerated. My uncles lived their lives going against the law. Drugs, violence, incarcerations and instability were everything they stood for, and Darnell and I were raised in that environment. Still, 501 was a house of hospitality, open to friends, family and all others sharing the same addiction.

I grew up vowing never to use drugs and hating dealers. Everyone in our house got high except for my grandmother and myself – my twin finally became a part of the generational curse of drug addiction in 1985. He always struggled in school, and once he began using, middle school was no longer in his daily routine. Along with his addiction came trouble with the law, sending him to jail for theft, distribution, possession of a narcotic and armed robbery. He was in and out of many different prison institutions, along with treatment and GED programs.

This became a long-time battle for my grandmother. Seeing her family succumb to the epidemic of our African American men, she worked hard every day with the hope of moving out of the projects, and by the time she did, they were already consumed by it all. It was not uncommon for the police to run into our house chasing my uncles or their friends or for them to be waiting outside the house with guns drawn in your face. My grandmother lost her first son in 1989 – my Uncle Milton was shot and murdered by his friend – and death seemed to overtake our family thereafter. Milton once robbed the Penn-doll Pharmacy while my grandmother, my brother and I were in the store getting her lottery ticket. He ran out of the store, took his mask off and came back in to get my grandmother like it hadn't been him.

We lost another uncle on July 26, 1991, Uncle Ronald, to AIDS from being an IV drug user. He was part of the ALIVE (AIDS Linked to IntraVenous Experiences) study at Johns Hopkins Hospital, which was a paid study that began in 1988. We believe he joined this study in the early 1990s, and it seems to have accelerated his condition, leaving him in a childlike state when he passed away. Other family members had the disease but their process was different. Uncle Ronald always kept a job – he worked for the city of Baltimore – but he blew his money regularly to support his drug habit. He was the compassionate one at times; I would see him lining people up on the side of the Stop Shop and Save to serve them testers for drugs.

My Uncle Larry died in February of 1995, while I was locked up. He was locked up himself for fifteen years, for killing the ice cream truck driver, but he wasn't guilty – another one of my uncles had committed the crime. After he came home, he eventually found out the truth and almost killed his brother for allowing him to take the fall for something his brother had done, but my grandmother intervened. Uncle Larry never really regained his life after that and kept going back and forth to jail, and that is where he died.

I still have one uncle who is incarcerated now and continues to battle all his demons. This was my life, and though it sounds sad and dangerous, my uncles were my physical protection; there are things that did not happen to me because of them. I remember when I was pregnant and I went outside to see why the police had my brother in custody at the side of my house. The policeman got in my face, hollering "get back," and touched my shoulder, but my uncles ran to the rescue and began to shout at the policeman, asking him if he was crazy for talking to me like that. Needless to say, my brother was no longer in custody and the policeman got in his car and drove off. They could not protect me from the men I would meet after their expiration, but I would come to know a protector like no other after a trail of pain.

The house at 501 was also filled with many memories of love, laughter, family and friendships. We gathered for Thanksgiving, for game night to play Pokeno and cards, and we often had house parties when we were young that ended with somebody fighting. It was good to see everyone together, being normal and allowing their personalities to be free. Even if it was temporary, it is a memory I hold dear to my heart, and when songs come on from the eighties like "Love Come Down," "Juicy Fruit," "Somebody Else's Guy," "Ain't Nobody" and "Forget Me Nots," just to name a few, I can see them laughing and dancing. Those memories are embedded forever, along with their jokes. But above all, the biggest thing my uncles represented in my life was protection.

My mother became the head of 501 when my grandmother moved to an apartment, but she bought her first house soon after, at 36 North Rosedale Street. It had its own share of pain. I inherited the gift of hair from my mother – she would do my hair, my grandmother's and her friends'. She never became licensed, but after leaving her warehouse job at Roper Easton after fifteen years, hair became her only income, outside of receiving welfare from the government. My mom enjoyed laughter, dancing, music and hanging out with a host of different friends. She had a temper and would cuss you out in a minute, then quickly recover, but if you crossed her, she would hold it against you and would express it. She had a habit of going upstairs with some of her friends and closing the door to her room for privacy. I did not know then but later found out from a bully who blurted it out to hurt me that she was doing syrup and pills. My response was, "My mother is not sick." Yes, I was a naïve little girl, but shortly after my brother confirmed it. My mother had us as twins at a young age while already dealing with her own insecurities in life, and she became addicted to drugs to escape the pain of her truths. Our lives seemed pretty normal to us until we were exposed to how others were raised outside of where we lived. Affection, hugs and kisses were not a part of 501, before school, after school or inside our home, so it was easy for me to misinterpret their meaning later in life. I can't recall hugs – a loud voice fussing and cussing was the way my mother showed her love and care.

My brother and I went to my paternal grandmother Mary's house every summer to spend time with that branch of our family, who loved us so much and displayed that love, but unfortunately my dad was always in prison. We can count the times we saw him on one hand after he and my mom broke up when we were about five years old. The most significant times I can remember were when he took my cousin Nikki and me to a New Edition concert and when he and my Uncle Al bought us toys and a Christmas tree on Christmas Eve. My grandmother Mary always cooked, and she worshiped God at church and even in her kitchen. We went to

Cahill Camp every summer and had many friends. We spent time with our Aunts Beverly and Cheneda, who loved us too, but not more than our Uncle Tony. We were loved by many, which we needed desperately, because affection was foreign to us from our parents.

We had many positive influences in our lives, even when we were home. We went to Sharp Street Church for Saturday Bible school, which gave all the kids in the neighborhood a chance to escape our normal lives, along with the Harvey Johnson Recreation Center and Church on the weekdays. They both taught us home economics and sports, but Sharp Street tutored us in reading and math. The most impactful was a woman named Mrs. Thomas, who taught me how to read every Tuesday at the Sharp Street Church Community Center, and I am forever grateful for her, as well as for First Lady Matthews and her daughter, who took me on a trip to Disney World. My grandmother provided most of the money to get me there – she always found ways to finance our exposure. The church was highly active and effective in the projects; they made a difference in all our lives.

I was afforded free opportunities exposing me to arts and other culture by way of modern dance. I began going to St. Mary's Park for dance sessions with a woman named Rhonda, who taught us how to express ourselves. I carried dance into middle school, where Mrs. Smith, our French teacher, also taught modern dance after school. Mrs. Smith, who did not play in either class, was a stern, strict teacher who was passionate about teaching and a love for dance. I was always able to accept the opportunities that were afforded to me. I joined the Baltimore Westsiders Marching Band in high school as I continued to express myself through dance and movement, and through traveling to march, I was exposed to other states. My cousin Antwon started his own marching band, the Baltimore Go-Getters, creating an outlet for all of us in the community where we could experience family, travel, fun, a release and something constructive to do. He also became a father figure for many of us who didn't have one in our home.

I had childhood friends, friends from school, friends from the club, from marching band, hair school, etc., which meant I was hanging out in many different areas – Pennsylvania Ave., CBS,

Murphy Homes, Bruce Manor and Cherry Hill, to name a few. In my teenage years, I had done more than your average young adult at twenty, but the emptiness inside and my behavior were truths I could not escape from. It was comfortable and safe for me to remain in poverty, but those experiences were deposits in my life that would one day come together and support who I would become.

Proverbs 27:3 KJV "For as he thinketh in his heart, so is he: Eat and drink, saith he to thee: But his heart is not with thee."

MY ADDICTION

According to Merriam-Webster, the definition of *addiction* is "a compulsive, chronic, physiological or psychological need for a habit-forming substance, behavior or activity."

The Word of God states in Exodus 34:7 (NIV) that the Lord is "maintaining love to thousands and forgiving wickedness, rebellion and sin. Yet he does not leave the guilty unpunished; he punishes the children and their children for the sin of the parents to the third and fourth generation," leaving us born into generational curses. Everyone has the power to create blessings from the curses that were passed down to them, but it takes faith, hope, strength, and the will of God to slay every Goliath we face to get to the other side. That is what my life was like – a battle to overcome on each level.

I was introduced to lust before entering the first grade, when a family member would play with my vagina and finger pop me. We would all be playing hide and seek, but I always seemed to be found and locked in a room for minutes that seemed like hours for them to violate me and my innocence. I didn't know it was wrong and thought it was part of the game until I witnessed it being done to my mother as she lay in our bed unconscious from her drug use, with me beside her. I did not understand what was happening, but I knew to keep my eyes closed as if I were asleep because of the person who was doing it. This was a different person, but I understood relationships enough to know that was wrong, and I locked them both in a place in my brain and heart that I never visited. What I didn't know was that those experiences would have lasting effects in my life. As a middle school student I would soon come to relive those feelings of lust that were introduced to me so young. They were awakened when we watched our first X-rated video before going to school while everyone was asleep and my grandmother had already left for work. Watching the videos fed the desire in me until I wanted the fulfillment. So there I was in the sixth grade, with no true understanding of the consequences of having sex for the first time, and as they say, getting my cherry busted. I thought that was the end of my desire until I learned the consequences of sex were pregnancy and the symptoms I was experiencing. We were watching a video in my social studies class on the reproductive system and what happens when women have babies – yes, I was pregnant at thirteen in the seventh grade and did not even know until I watched that video.

We never had conversations in my family about our cycles, sex and what to expect, so I never knew what could happen until I found myself trying to figure out how to tell my mother. Then my great-grandmother Mama Sis started having dreams of fish. Our elders always believed when they dreamed of fish, someone in the family was pregnant – the fish represented an embryo thriving within the amniotic fluid. She asked me one day why she had not seen any sanitary napkins in the trash, and I told her what I had done.

The two things I remember most are how furious my mother was and how frightened I was to get an abortion at that age. I was past the point of the pregnancy where the process is simplest and had to get a more invasive procedure instead – they had to insert suppositories in me every hour until I delivered the fetus. Now, writing this from the perspective of a mature woman with two daughters, I realize for the first time how intense that was for a thirteen-year-old. I cannot imagine it for my own daughters.

You would have thought that would have scared me straight and it would have been the last time that would take place, but it seemed as though sex had introduced me to an affection which was never practiced in my childhood. I felt I had no need for protection because it made me feel loved – landing me in the same situation a second time. I borrowed my friends' dirty sanitary napkins to put them in the trash cans in my house to throw off Mama Sis, and I stole my medical care card out of my mother's purse to get another abortion. I had a friend's sister act as my older sibling to give authorization during my initial appointment prior to the actual abortion. The day of the procedure, instead of going to middle school, I prepared to walk to University Hospital, and had to duck behind the apartments on Pennsylvania Avenue because my mother was walking up the street and almost saw me – a close call. I made it to my appointment, and when I was released from recovery, I was put in a cab straight to my girlfriend's house. I took a nap to rest my body and returned home around six o'clock as if nothing ever happened.

Somehow, I still didn't take the risk seriously until I got pregnant again and had to get another abortion. This time my mother was involved with the consent, and when they went through my history to confirm that it was my third abortion, she looked at me and saw my face and as soon as the nurse left the room, I got cussed out. Yet still I never looked at the consequences as being serious until the fifth and last time, which was years later, in my relationship with a man named Tre. My two daughters were thirteen and ten, my life was different, my relationship with the Lord was growing and the consequences of my actions became an overwhelming weight. I had come to realize that I was choosing to end life that God had given me because of my ignorance, selfishness and immaturity. I wavered back and forth over my options. I was in a relationship with another broken being who had four kids of his own already, I had two, and I was taking care of my household with little to no help and only five years into my career, so after weeks of sobbing and crying out to God in repentance and asking forgiveness for not learning to protect myself, I decided to have an abortion one last time, committing that I would never put myself in that position again. I made that decision on my own without consulting the father, who already had his hands full with his four, and that was the end of me abusing life, my body and a woman's choice of abortion.

So, my addiction was not drugs, which was common to the generations of my family. Yet sex as a habit had the same result of leading to daily decisions that had the potential to affect me for the rest of my life or even be deadly. Sexually transmitted diseases and AIDS were the two risks I most worried about. I had seen the effects of AIDS in our community and in my immediate family, and the deterioration it causes in the body, losing weight, strength and hair, was so sad to witness, but that fear wasn't enough to cause me to protect myself. I just didn't have enough self-love for that. I was addicted to the temporary feelings of being caressed, being wanted and all the lies of lust that make you feel loved. This addiction was the way I began all my encounters with men; it was the way I came to know dating. If I did not have a regular encounter to call, I would not miss the opportunity of a one-night stand. I would flirt with people until it landed me a number I could use to get what I wanted, and I always succeeded. Lust is a never-ending drive that leads you to places you never thought you would be, searching with an unquenchable desire that is never fulfilled. Lust was the feeling that made me believe I was wanted, valuable enough to want and good enough to keep, and it was better than being alone dealing with pain.

Music and dancing defined my weekends. The Baltimore club life was an escape from the reality of my life, and I was there every weekend beginning at age fourteen. It started at Shake & Bake, Godfrey's and Paradox with my childhood friends, then expanded to Odell's, Whitten's and Volcanoes, just to name a few. I always had a group of girls to party with from different neighborhoods. My favorite drinks were the Long Island iced tea and the adios motherfucker – you can only imagine how those drinks made me feel. I would drink when I entered the club and start to sober up by the time we left, which meant I would be driving my grandmother's car under the influence, falling asleep at red lights and speeding, but God covered me.

When I started high school, things were a little different because my clique changed from females to males. I guess I wanted to learn how to understand men and how they thought, but they just became guys I laughed and hung out with. I also became the class clown. I had finally found a way to be the center of attraction. Laughing and joking was another way to release all the realities of my life. It relieved the pressure.

I fell into a pattern of unprotected sex – and to think, I had a boyfriend named Wan in school who always wanted to spend time with me, introduced me to his family and had me over after school, but never tried to have sex. For that reason, I kept him separate from what I was doing at home. At the same time, I was also talking to a guy named Kit, another sexual partner from my neighborhood who had left and enlisted in the Army. He wasn't going to help my addiction either, so while I communicated with them I was always searching for someone to take care of my habit. In fact I had two sexual encounters with the man I found, and on the first one I became pregnant. I was getting tired of these encounters, even though they afforded us both the opportunity of pleasure consistently, and at times I felt used and began to desire more. The lack of protection finally caught up with me, and with a yearning to be loved and to have someone love me, I decided to keep this pregnancy. So, while other girls were being celebrated by their parents with a sweet sixteen, I came to a halt in my life of promiscuity in exchange for motherhood. I delivered my first daughter one month prior to my seventeenth birthday.

Latia Cherise Milburn was born on October 21st, 1990, at 7 lbs., 9 oz. She would indeed come to love me unconditionally, and I would learn the true meaning of love through parenting. Her dad and I were cordial but never in a relationship, and though I wanted him to be a good father, he was married to the street life until the poison he sold to others became his own addiction. My daughter became my saving grace, leading me to slow down my destructive behavior, but little did I know that she would repeat my same mistakes because I chose a father for her just like mine, who only spent time with her on a handful of occasions and whose addiction was more important to him. She was my fourth pregnancy but the first I carried to term, as a junior in high school. I was a lost little girl searching for love and a father by way of lust, and I had made the decision to keep her because I thought she would love me unconditionally and never leave me. What a terrible thing to put on a child – though so many young girls make the same decisions. I learned over time that was not a reason to bring life into this world, but it was a great reason for me to become the woman I never knew existed. My addiction was no longer a priority, but a desire to be in a relationship accompanied the lust and blinded me to the red flags within each person.

I made it to my senior year in school. I had gone to my junior prom alone and now I was seeking to enjoy prom night with someone who would pay for all my expenses, and I had less than four months to find him. One of my girlfriends' cousins would always flash his money around and show interest in me, but I did not like him – still, he was at the top of the list for exactly what I wanted and more. We got to talking, and before you knew it we were hanging out and spending time together while my mother watched my daughter. Prom came around and he paid for my pictures and dinner, and you already know what happened next, but this time it was the beginning of a relationship.

I was beginning to think my life was looking better – I was almost finished with school, and my mother and my brother's girlfriend Nicole helped me with Latia while I was in class or hanging out at the baseball game afterward. Nicole was pregnant with my nephew, Darnell Jr. at the time but she allowed me to have a life afterschool and on the weekend by keeping Tia until I returned home. RIP Nicole Keith, I always loved her for that, despite addiction being a struggle within her life. But soon my surroundings reminded me of my reality. My twin was in and out of jail like my dad, my mother and uncles were still addicts, and our house was raided again. This time my daughter was present. It was a wakeup call for me that my daughter's childhood was about to mimic mine, and I vowed to change. To stop her childhood repeating my own, I moved out at the age of eighteen and got my own apartment. I wanted a different life for my daughter… yet I was moving with a drug dealer.

Psalm 46:1: NLT God is our refuge and strength, always ready to help in times of trouble.

A BROKEN PROMISE

I promised myself I would never use drugs – I saw what they did to my family and how they controlled their lives – yet I still managed to be involved with a dealer who profited from the addictions of others. I had my very first apartment, 2305 Round Road in Cherry Hill, and I thought I was grown. My entire income was my social service check, a total of $372 a month, and my rent was $342 with gas and electricity. I could not afford the place, but with my boyfriend I had nothing to worry about, or so I thought. I enjoyed the luxury of clothes, hanging out, eating what I wanted and going to concerts and driving different cars, but it all came at a price. It was introducing me to a lifestyle I was not legally working to afford.

My daughter Latia did not like being around my boyfriend. She would cry so hard when it was time to go home. She did not like his spirit. And what did I do as a mother? Instead of looking at my daughter's feelings as a warning, I let her stay at my mother's and only come home on the weekends. I didn't know I was teaching her the same thing my mother had taught me, that my dysfunctional relationship was more important than her. How did I trust her to be with a drug addict, how did I leave her in the place I had wanted so desperately to flee? I guess deep down inside I knew the environment I was providing was no different.

I had been so ready to move into my first apartment to protect my daughter from my life that I jumped into a situation that was just a different version of where I'd come from. I recall moving and feeling so good that I had control over who came over to our house. My daughter finally had her own room and I felt like a woman, but eventually the novelty wore off and I succumbed to my environment. I was helping my boyfriend package drugs, make deliveries and even get over on people. When he was home it was good. We laughed together, ate together, watched movies and, most important, we were friends. But there was a filter on our relationship – it looked happy from the outside, but there were many sleepless nights that stemmed from the hustle, cheating and arguing. When I didn't know where he was and he wasn't answering my calls, I knew there were other women, from the repeated phone calls or limited conversation, perfume smells and constant lies for no reason. I knew who he was, and I was beginning to think he would never change. We became less intimate as time went on, and I still had to mask my feelings of unhappiness and loneliness.

I often asked myself how I had gotten into this situation, but I was trying to create a different life for myself. I got a job working at a convenience store for a truly kind employer who helped me out as much as he could. I had to be at work at eight a.m., which meant catching the bus to my mother's to drop my daughter off, then catching another bus to work. All while my boyfriend had a car – clearly he did not care enough to pick me up in the morning. He would claim he was working all night. I found someone from Cherry Hill to watch Latia, which saved me the bus to my mom's, but it was winter and though my boyfriend had gotten me a lambskin coat, I was still at the bus stop in the snow and pushing my daughter in the stroller to the babysitter's house. He finally got me a car for my birthday, my first car, a tan Toyota Cressida, and I was so excited I forgot about all the pain I was living in just for a moment. I got my driver's license the next day, a Friday. I went to work, had my fun over the weekend, went joy riding to see my girlfriends, and Monday in the wee hours of the morning, I heard a big bang. I looked out my window to see my precious new car burning in flames! We never found out who did it – there was talk of a dirty cop – but that was when I began to fear the lifestyle I had chosen for myself and my daughter.

To intensify it all, I was pregnant with my second child. The dirty cop, named Carter, was beginning to knock on our door and ask me questions, and in the same month our apartment got raided. I was eight months pregnant and had an asthma attack when I came home from work to find my house a mess and the police rummaging through my things. As soon as they'd finished questioning me, I left. Of course my boyfriend was nowhere to be found. I caught a hack to my mother's and stayed there until he and I got another apartment a month later.

The police filed possession charges against me for finding drug paraphernalia. My boyfriend tried to take the charge, but the apartment was in my name, so they charged me. When I went to court to answer those charges, they put it on a stet, which means that if I were to be charged with the same thing again in the future, they could bring those charges back up.

A fresh start seemed like it was ahead of us, but our new place at 2811 Virginia Avenue had its own share of problems. We were hanging together during the day, but when I went back to the apartment at night, he would say his famous line, "I be back." It seemed I was living all by myself. We spent a Sunday at his brother's house, and it was close to my due date, so instead of him dropping me off home by myself I insisted on going to my mother's. Thank God I listened to my intuition, because I woke up at eight in the morning in active labor. I called him again and again but got no answer, so I then called my great-grandmother, who lived in the senior high-rise building ten yards away, and asked for money to catch a hack to the hospital. She brought the money to me and I was in the hack within twenty minutes of that phone call. I told my mother what was happening and asked her to keep trying to reach my boyfriend. I got to the hospital around nine o'clock, and I delivered my second daughter, Tykira Chanel Ceaser, 8 lbs.,

1 oz, on April 2, 1993 at 11:04 a.m. Though I was alone during the labor, he finally showed up, but I didn't allow that drama to overshadow the gift that I had just birthed. His sister had already planned a baby shower at his mom's house for that Saturday, so when I was released from the hospital I went to her house in Cherry Hill for the shower. I stayed for two weeks before I returned home.

We were toxic for one another, and after six months we were fighting like a cat and dog. One time when his sister and a girlfriend of hers were over at our apartment, he was on the phone with a female buddy of his, but I knew he was messing with her friend, and I felt like he was disrespecting me in front of the company. I told him to get off the phone, and when his friend on the line started saying something slick, he allowed it and became verbally disrespectful when I said something about it, so I jumped up to snatch the phone out of his hand and banged him in his face. We were fist fighting while our guests were trying to break it up, and when the police arrived they thought the company was fighting and not me, since they were all tousled-looking. On another occasion we had an argument and I asked my girlfriend Tee-Tee to pick me up. He pulled up behind her and as I gave her Tykira to get in the car he kicked her door, shattering the glass all over the interior. How did verbal and physical abuse become acceptable and normal in my relationship? It was because we both were filled with anger that had not yet become evident to us and had no one to help us process the pain. I finally made the decision to leave him when he put a hole in the wall and broke the glass on our dining room table. I moved back home again to 501 Hoffman Street.

My twin was always out of jail when I needed to move home. My second time moving back, it was summer. We had broken up but eventually we were back together again. When I went to look for my coats and the kids' collection of Barney videos, my brother had sold it all. It crushed me and I was angry with him for years, so much so I decided not to visit him again when he went back to jail. Besides, I was tired of visiting every prison institution because of his decisions. Some of the correctional officers, especially the women, would keep me waiting longer than usual because they would assume I was his wife instead of his sister, given we had the same name, and they obviously had something going on. He would confirm that for me after the fact.

It was evident I had also become addicted to pain and punishment, living in an even greater whirlwind than at Hoffman Street. I got a job working as a Christmas casual at the post office and moved out again to a house in the 2700 block of Harlem Ave. so we could be together again. When the post office job was over, I started working at my boyfriend's sister's salon as an assistant, finally doing what I had a passion to do. I still found time to go out and party on the weekends to ease the reality of my life. What little beliefs and values I had were no longer visible. I had been consumed by the darkness I had lived in for five years, and despite my hopes of changing it, I got sucked back in. When you don't have the ability to stop the destruction in your life but God values your life, He finds a way to shut it down.

Proverbs 2:13–14 (NLT): "These men turn from the right way to walk down dark paths."

IMPRISONMENT

It was November 1st, 1994, my twenty-first birthday. I woke up with knots in my stomach as I prepared for my court appearance at Clarence M. Mitchell Jr. Courthouse to stand trial on charges of distribution of marijuana. That day, I was sentenced to seven months in prison by Judge John Prevas and sent to the Jessup Correctional Institution for Women.

I can still hear my grandmother crying out "Nooo!" in the courtroom, weeping. I was the only granddaughter, the good girl, and the generations of drugs, violence and incarceration were not supposed to affect my life. Not to mention that Judge Prevas was the same judge who had previously sentenced two of my uncles to prison. Seven months may not sound like a long time, but I had never been away from my daughters Latia and Tykira, who were three years and one year of age. As dysfunctional as our family was, I would miss our holiday gathering for Thanksgiving and Christmas, and this was not how I had intended to spend my birthday. And lastly, my mother was dying of AIDS.

How did I get here? I had been offered an opportunity by a family member of my boyfriend to make a substantial amount of money just by receiving packages of marijuana delivered by UPS. My boyfriend knew nothing about my side dealings – I told him I was getting the money from my grandmother because she had hit the lottery – and I kept it that way until it all blew up. During my sophomore year in high school, I used to live with my Aunt Faye, who worked at the Department of Juvenile Justice, and I still had a key. I used her house to receive the deliveries, and I would call my contact once the packages were delivered, using an alias. When someone came to pick them up, usually a Jamaican guy, I got paid. Easy money, right? It seemed so simple and harmless, but I never counted the cost or the consequences until I had no other choice. My character was assassinated. So many people I thought loved me created and spread lies about me, and my freedom was taken away. I did not realize I was putting the lives of my family members in jeopardy until it all fell apart. I accepted marijuana shipments through UPS multiple times, and though I was nervous every time, I enjoyed spending the money on my daughters or the house. Everything went smoothly until the connection switched up the shipping method and the packages were intercepted by the feds.

I remember the details as if it were yesterday. The packages were supposed to come that Friday and never showed up. On Saturday, I got a call from my cousin saying packages were delivered for me. I had never mentioned what I was doing to anybody, so from that moment I had an uneasy feeling about the pickup. Still, I proceeded as planned.

There were a lot of cars on the street and in the alley, which was unusual, and I sat in the car contemplating for a moment, wondering if I should go in. But my cousin was now involved in something he knew nothing about, so I had to. When I walked in the house, my cousin was sitting on the couch looking like a statue, with this blank look on his face, and the basement door was open, which was always closed. As my anxiety grew, I asked, "What's wrong? And why is the basement door open?" As he nodded to say "nothing," I walked in the kitchen, looked out the window, saw no people and just decided it would be less obvious to take the bricks out of the boxes and put them in bags. The moment I opened the boxes, this tall white man walked out of the basement, and I just looked at my cousin, thinking, "Damnnn" as he looked at me in disbelief. If I had listened to my spirit, then he would have gotten in trouble for something he wasn't involved in at all.

So they asked questions, and I told them I didn't know anything about the person but a name and a number to contact for them to pick the package up, and that was my first time opening a delivery. They had me page him – we used pagers back then – and wait for the call, but when the Jamaican called back, I called him another name so he would know something was wrong. The police wanted me to tell him my car broke down and to meet me at the gas station so they would get him instead of me – they knew that I was just a small part of this operation. I knew he would not show up, so I sat in my car in anxiety and fear, hanging halfway out onto Hanover Street from the Amoco gas station with my hazard lights on while the police waited at a pump. I had a panic attack while we waited, plus I had to go to the bathroom. After an hour, the police came to the car to say, "I guess no one is going to show up, so we have to charge you." They put me in handcuffs and drove me to Central Bookings, and my car was sent to the city pound. It was the longest weekend of my life, locked up, not knowing if my life was in danger from the Jamaicans who didn't get their package or what the consequences would be for me. At the time they were known to do all kinds of things to people who messed up their drug money, so I was afraid. But on Monday, the family member of my boyfriend who had gotten me involved in all this provided a lawyer and posted my bail, and everything seemed fine until my life began to change.

The people I trusted and who had trusted me were no more. I had to come clean to my boyfriend, telling him where I had really been getting the money and who was involved. I had eight months until my court date, and the closer it got, the more I prepared for the worst. I knew that there were lies going around that I was snitching and reporting to the police, and though it hurt me, I ignored it. None of it was true, and if it were, I would not have been preparing for the unknown. There were so many people I called friends, but only two showed up after court – the officer at the courthouse lockup told me I had two friends in the hall crying and asking him to tell me they loved me. It turned out to be Lashawn and Sherri.

After I counted the cost, it was not worth jeopardizing my aunt's career and my future, disappointing my grandmother and feeling so alone with the guilt and regret of what I had done because every decision I made had a direct effect on my daughters. I also grew hate in my heart toward the people who were involved and wanted bad things to happen to them, so they would feel the pain I felt.

The enemy had celebrated the victory of another dream intercepted by the generational curse. The curses are the same, but the effects on each generation are different. I cried a whole week in prison, wondering why me, filled with anger, and missing my daughters and my boyfriend – who was in an awkward position but never wavered in his support of me, at least not until I was gone. I had to wait until my medicals were cleared before they could put me in population with the other inmates, and that gave me time to get my emotions together for the unknown journey ahead, not knowing what that would entail.

So this was the point when the previous charges that were put on a stet came back to haunt me. It was my second drug offense. This made me a security risk, so they classified me into a secure building until my court date. What I remember most is the ride to the court – they put shackles on my feet and shackles on my hands that connected to the handcuffs, and that was humiliating. I did enjoy the ride outside of jail, but it was just for a moment. They decided on a nolle prosequi for the previous charges, and that case was over. But I still had to face the consequences of the second charge.

When I stepped onto A-Wing, I was terrified to learn it housed mostly murderers and people with long-term sentencing. Still, my roommate turned out to be cool. She was from PG County, in for a ten-year drug charge, and though she was fickle, we did not have issues. God also sent me a like-spirited person to connect with whose husband had gone to the store to get milk and robbed it without her knowing while she was in the car. We encouraged each other during our time. We went to the gym or recreation every day and walked around listening to Mary J. Blige's *My Life*. That album got us through our imprisonment, and she also represented victory over a dark past and addiction.

When they moved me from A-Wing, I finally had a set place to rest in. My new roommate was an older woman named Priscilla, who introduced me to reading books and the Bible. Aside from school, I had never really read books – not as leisure or for growth – so that was a big deal to me. It connected me back to an inner peace and a knowledge that everything would be okay. I started working in the kitchen, which meant I had to wake up at four o'clock to be there by 4:30 to prepare breakfast trays and deliver them at six. I'd repeat the routine for lunch, then I was off.

The reality of being cut off from the outside world and your freedom being taken away was intense, and the only thing that kept me hopeful each day was receiving mail and visitors. I had many friends during that time but only three came to see me – Sherri, Lashawn and Tee-Tee. I often got mail and money orders from my grandmother without asking, but Tee-Tee also wrote and sent pictures. I saw my daughters one time, during a Christmas special visit. The children stayed for two hours. I told them I was in school and the officers were school security. They were confused and didn't know how to feel, and I held back those emotions for their whole visit. I cried for hours after, and that was the last time I wanted to see them – it took me days to get myself together emotionally.

When my boyfriend came to see me, a girl I worked with in the kitchen got hyped about him in the visiting room, saying, "Oh my God, that's your boyfriend?" I asked him what the deal was, saying I needed him to tell me the truth before she did at work. But he said nothing, and I realized that his drama had followed me to prison. I got up and walked away, abandoning the visit, and that was the last time I wanted to see him. The next morning, I found out he had another full relationship with her cousin, and the details she gave me added up – including an engagement ring that I did not accept, which he then gave to her. She described the ring in detail. So I finally had proof that he was cheating on me, and offering someone else a ring that I had rejected meant he was serious about her. After my friends Sherri and LaShawn's visit, in which they cried the whole time, I refused all visits and stopped calling home regularly. I had to cut myself off from the people I loved, because I lived in a place where survival mode was void of emotions. Emotions could cost you more than you imagined in prison, so I had to just embrace my situation.

In the five months and twenty-nine days I spent in prison, I had time to redirect my focus back to God and to make plans to go to school for hair to pursue my passion. I began the process of forgiveness, and I was eliminating people from my life who did not positively affect me or show me I was of value to them. The only people who have always been consistent and who made sure I had money in my commissary and packages during the holidays were my grandmother and her friends from work. My daughters were separated most of the time, but I have always been grateful for Mrs. Sissy, who watched Tykira while I worked in the salon as an assistant, and during my incarceration, along with my mother (may they both rest in heaven) for taking care of my daughters and nurturing them in my absence. God provides, even during your pain.

Hebrews 12:11 (ESV): "For the moment all discipline seems painful rather than pleasant, but later it yields the peaceful fruit of righteousness to those who have been trained by it."

FREEDOM AND LOSS

It was my release day! I was released from prison in March 1995, and it was time for another chance at life. I had learned so much about myself and the people who genuinely loved me and showed up for me. I had created a plan in jail for when I returned home: to keep growing my relationship with God, to continue to forgive myself and others, to let go of unhealthy relationships and the people who were not supportive to my valley season, to find my passion and purpose, and to never return to prison. I began to implement them one by one.

The more I learned about myself, the more I was successful in growing. I chose not to move back into the house on Harlem Ave. with my boyfriend after my release. He and I still cared about each other and messed around, but things were not the same after what I had learned about him while incarcerated. Instead I went back to 501 Hoffman Street.

It took me a lot of adjusting to building a relationship with my daughters and living back in the McCulloh Homes Projects, but I tried to enjoy the time I had left with my mother. I spent five months with her during her illness, having conversations we'd never had and telling her all the things she'd never known about me. We celebrated her birthday and Mother's Day and worshipped together on Easter. It was still a battle, because she could not operate for a day without using drugs – they were her only way to get out of bed as her body and weight declined. I thought I was preparing myself, but you cannot prepare yourself for death until it happens. I went to visit my mother on Monday, and she looked well, as if she were getting better, but her talking about how she saw family members who were deceased did not escape me. After the visit, with apprehension, I took the girls to New York for a parade with the Go-Getters marching band. The girls and I had so much fun, and when the bus arrived back in Baltimore, my boyfriend was there to pick us up. He was very quiet on the ride home. When we pulled up, I asked, "Why are all these cars at the house?", and he said, "You know why. Your mother is gone." I got out of the car and screamed at the top of my lungs as the guilt of leaving to go to New York overtook me. My mother passed away on September 17th, 1995. She had an addiction to drugs and had contracted AIDS from her boyfriend, who was still living at the time of her death, which infuriated me. A part of me was glad she was no longer suffering, but I was never prepared to live a life motherless as a twenty-one-year-old.

Our relationship was not your typical mother–daughter, but I learned to appreciate all that she contributed to my life over years visiting her gravesite. I had to navigate a lifetime of emotions about my childhood, her lifelong battle with her addiction and how it had affected me. The process of appreciation began after I saw the movie *Antwone Fisher*, about a man whose mother had abandoned him and he never met her. Thinking about that helped me find truths that allowed me to relinquish some of those emotions that had controlled my own addiction. My mother made sure we ate meals and combed our hair, she disciplined us, we had a curfew, we spent time laughing and hanging out with her friends' children, and she never openly exposed us to her addiction. I never actually saw her get high. She had given us all that she had, excluding affection. She loved us the best way she knew how and kept her addiction out of our sight. The one thing that haunted me was that I supported her through the drug treatment process at least three times and I had hopes that the last time would be it, until her boyfriend was released from jail and he sent her on a downward spiral again. Her actions always spoke loud to me. Even as I began to make peace with our relationship, I couldn't shake the feeling that I was never good enough for my mother to choose me over her addiction.

I was happy her suffering was over but was not prepared to live without the woman who had carried me in her womb for nine months. Mr. Green, the undertaker, frequently visited our house during the preparation for the funeral. I volunteered to style her hair, because she had always done her own hair and had taught me, so I knew that she wouldn't have wanted anybody else to do it. It gave me temporary comfort and peace that I had a chance to present her in the beauty that I had known her in prior to life's battles – a chance to finally see her free. It gave me a reason to maintain my emotions. The grief had not fully kicked in yet. Mr.

Green asked me twice if I was sure I could do this, but I was certain. I would make my mother's last appearance on earth a great one. When we went to the funeral home for the family hour, a private viewing for the family to approve her body going on public view, Mr. Green asked me, "Did you do your mother's hair?" I answered that I had, and he complimented me on how well I had done – and offered me a job.

After the funeral, my brother's name was the only one associated with the house, so housing put in a transfer for a one-bedroom unit, and that meant it was time for me to leave 501 without an option to return. I tried everything possible to keep the property. One of the church members from Sharp Street asked Keiffer J. Mitchell, who was the councilman of Baltimore City at the time and whose family were also members, to help me, and he got me an appointment with Reginald Scriber, the head of the Housing Authority of Baltimore City, which was my last hope. When I met with Mr. Scriber, he told me that "his hands were tied." He went on to explain that there are times when honesty will do that – I had been honest about the felony on my record, and housing no longer allowed people with felony records to obtain public housing units. It was devastating news to learn that my mistakes were proving a hindrance on my life. I came home one day in October and my brother had moved most of the furniture to his own apartment, across the street from 501 in Stoddard Court. The time had come to move. I was stricken with grief again. I cried so much that day. I called my ex-boyfriend to come be with me, and he said he was coming right away. Well, it was two o'clock in the morning when I called my grandmother to come get me because I couldn't stop crying and the thought of never returning was so painful. That was the last time I entertained running back to my boyfriend. I finally realized that he was a man who provided but never showed me protection, and because I was grieving my mother and losing 501, it penetrated to the core. Looking back, the loss of 501 was a blessing. It forced me out of the familiar poverty of the projects and into a life I had not yet known.

That was also the death of my dysfunctional, abusive rollercoaster of a relationship. I later found out that my ex-boyfriend had sold all my furniture, which I had purchased for our

Harlem Avenue house using the money from my illegal dealings, after lying to me that it was in storage. That was the ultimate betrayal, to find out he had taken from me after such a great loss in my life, which validated my decision never to look back when it came to him.

I was now living with my grandmother and dealing with grief. It was the best place for my children and me to be, because I was emotionally unavailable to my daughters. I had started working at Kmart when I was released and later got a job at North American Beauty Warehouse, but the pain of losing my mother affected my performance, so I quit. I decided it was finally time to pursue my cosmetology career. Mr. Green gave me a reason to enroll at the Baltimore Studio of Hair Design to obtain my cosmetology certification to provide hair services for the deceased, but I soon realized that I was purposed to minister this gift to the living. The pain of prison and death had pushed me to stay true to my plan and become a cosmetologist. Still, in my grief I would relapse into my old behavior on the weekends, partying, drinking and having sex again as a way to find comfort. School was my priority, but my weekends were out of control. I had a live-in babysitter and the freedom to go as I pleased, and I took full advantage of that with my grandmother. It got so bad I would invite people to her house and we would be in the basement while she and my daughters were on the third floor sleeping. I never saw that I was disrespecting her home, until I had matured. Years later we had a conversation about me being out of control. I asked her, "Why didn't you stop me?" Her response was, "I knew you were grieving and I didn't know what to do to help you." Still, I was working hard in cosmetology school. Some days I would even stay for night classes, which allowed me to finish the course two months early. I felt accomplished to have a chance to operate my gift on a level my mother was never able to reach. It would be for both of us.

    I was ready to begin my career, but my personal life was still a wreck. Realizing that pushed me to take control and continue to carry out my dreams. I mailed off my papers to take my state board exam to become a cosmetologist. I passed the test and was awaiting my license, but what I received was a letter saying that because of my criminal record, I had to appear before a board to prove that I was fit to serve the public. Can you imagine what that felt like? Ten months of school, following through on my plan after jail, and now it may all have been for nothing. It was a nerve-racking two weeks. During the hearing they asked me several questions and told me they would give me their answer that same day. But I trusted that I had done something right for myself and that I could defend myself as the new woman I was becoming. The consequences of my actions reached into every corner of my life, but they did not stop me from becoming a licensed cosmetologist in February 1999.

"God intentionally allows you to go through painful experiences to equip you for ministry to others." – Rick Warren

Psalm 34:18 (MSG): "If your heart is broken, you'll find God right there; if you're kicked in the gut, he'll help you catch your breath."

THE CROSSROADS

When I left prison, I set out on a journey to choose a different road in life than the one I had been driving. The five things I focused on after my incarceration were now showing results – so far, in the areas of forgiveness and self-love, finding my passion and creating a safe home for myself and my daughters. When I ended the relationship with my boyfriend after being released from prison, I didn't want to be associated with anything that could potentially put me back in that position and I knew he would always be a womanizer, so I sought to make changes in that area of my life to create a safe environment for my daughters. I began working in my passion at a premiere salon as soon as I got my license, and this career would be the catalyst to my growth and a place where I would meet examples of women I had never known. The employees and clients at the salon were a different class of woman, outside the comfort zone of my poverty. Seeing this, I concentrated on my work and on listening to conversations that inspired me to embrace something new. I began to grow.

The owner of the salon became my mentor. She taught me so much that I began to look at her as a mother figure and valued her guidance. My clientele as a hairstylist grew so much within two years that it afforded me the opportunity to purchase my dream home at the age of thirty on July 27th, 2001. My daughters and I moved to 3813 Fernhill Avenue on August 1st. It was an old single-family house with a driveway, a porch and a big backyard for the girls to enjoy. I had succeeded in entering a level of life that my mother had never known, though I did grieve the previous one from time to time.

Most of my relationships had changed, but my poverty mindset followed me, and all the good things happening in my life weren't enough to stop me from falling back into my old addiction to sex and bad relationships. I had crossed over into a new era of my life, but my behavior did not change. Give a million dollars to a junkie and see how long they last before the money is gone. I had just spent five years in a relationship with Wan, the guy I'd been in love with in high school who wanted a relationship but wouldn't have sex, who I'd stopped talking to when I became pregnant. It broke his heart when he found out. When we met up eight years later, we started a new relationship that was sexually fulfilling, and he spent a lot of time with me. I soon discovered, though, that he had no drive to build a career or even buy his own car – he always wanted to drive mine while I was at work. He also lived with his family and never had any intention of moving, since he had the basement to himself. I couldn't love him beyond his weed habit and I wasted five years going nowhere fast. After the first two years it was clear to me that it was time to go, but I somehow became comfortable with having a man around. "He spends time with me," I thought all the time, "so surely he loves me." But it was a lie I taught myself because being present with me was something my father had neglected, and I wasted time listening to the lies of a little girl instead of my intuition as a woman.

That relationship ended before I started the process of buying my home. I was beginning to learn what bondage looked like, and when I was free from it, I had the strength to do anything I set my mind to. I had three to four months clean before I picked up another sexual habit, a new friends-with-benefits relationship with no commitment. I was in search of a man who wanted to marry me, but I had not yet come to know who I was, so I kept entertaining flesh connections that couldn't last. This was an older guy who was married, another drug dealer. We both enjoyed the sexual chemistry, and it grew into feelings but never a relationship. But old habits never die, and here I was expecting something from nothing. It lasted about a year. He gave me money while I was saving all my income for the house, but once I realized that he had never left his wife, I was heartbroken again. I didn't get out of bed for two days, sick and tired of broken relationships and looking for a way to break the cycle.

God had blessed my daughters and me in two areas of my life, my career and our home, and still I managed to taint it by carrying my old mindset and addictive behavior with me.

I was turning a new leaf but operating in old habits. I met my next boyfriend, Tre, at a party while hanging out with my salon co-workers. He seemed different and kind-spirited. We talked a lot on the phone but never went on a date – just as well, since the type of date I usually had was no different than the other dessert! This felt good. We spent a lot of time together, my daughters liked him, and eventually he moved with me. We were playing house with his four kids every other week and my two – that meant providing a lot of food! Some difficult interactions, arguments, discomfort and unemployment were among the challenges we had in our relationship, but he went to church and worshipped God, and that was our greatest connection. When we started to talk about marriage, I asked if we could start going out on dates with us and the kids, and he agreed. He was also training for a new job that would allow him to contribute consistently in the household.

When my cousin invited me to her anniversary party, it was our chance to go out on a free date and for him to show me that what was important to me was also important to him, but he didn't come home in time to go with me to the party. I was devastated. It was like my father abandoning me all over again. The next day we had a heated argument that we could not recover from. Things were said that could not be taken back. That relationship had lasted for about four years, and I grieved it for another year until we finally had a conversation that bought me closure.

I tried again with a guy named Tony, who was divorced. He treated me well, worked, cooked dinner and invited me to places with his family, but everything was his way and all of our dates were at his home. He never wanted to spend money on me or accepted invitations from me to hang out at events, and when I invited him to go to the Poconos with me, my treat, he didn't even offer to drive back. Things became clearer, and I decided I had spent enough time with his selfishness, so that ended within a year. I was beginning to pay attention to the red flag a lot earlier than before.

I finally came to a place of discovering myself and learned to be okay with treating myself the way I wanted a man to treat me. I began to create standards that I would not compromise on for the men I entertained – a relationship with God, his own place, a job, dates, treating me better than I treat myself and a connection with my daughters. By holding to these standards, I knew I could finally turn the corner and leave my generational curse behind for good.

Romans 12:2 (NLT): "Don't copy the behavior and customs of this world, but let God transform you into a new person by changing the way you think. Then you will learn to know God's will for you, which is good and pleasing and perfect."

PARENTAL INFLUENCE

Parenthood is the most imperative and beneficial role a person can ever embark upon in this lifetime. We introduce our infants to the world, we nurture them, teach them, raise them, influence them and introduce them to life as we know it to be, and that can impact their lives in a negative or positive way. We are their first god. You are your child's greatest influence! And never doubt that the saying "they do as they see and not as you say" has been proven repeatedly. My parents affected me tremendously, but ultimately, I had to decide to reject the negative and learn a new way by understanding their pain had consumed them and they could only love me in the limited capacity that they had learned to love themselves.

When both your parents battle with addiction to drugs and your dad spends his entire life in and out of prison and abuses women, you grow up without seeing anything that can teach you how to invest in your adulthood. Underneath it all were two individuals who made repeated decisions to self-destruct, consumed by the power of their pain. While I know that they both loved me to their own measure of love, it was not enough to prepare me for life or protect me from all the evil forces that were manifesting due to their lack of self-love, violations of trust, immaturity and the generational curses from those who had preceded them in our family.

My mother already had the disadvantage of being the fourth of six children, feeling neglected by a mother who had no alternative but to work long hours to supply meals and a home for them all. She began her battle with alcohol while partying and then it progressed into drugs, all while she was being sexually fondled and inappropriately touched by a close family friend. I was witnessing these acts while my twin brother and I were asleep in the same bed as toddlers. When she spoke out about it, nothing was done, so she suffered in silence, and the self-destructive behavior became an influence to me in my life.

My father was the middle of five children, raised in a Christian home by two parents. The lack of attention and time came from his father, who worked countless hours outside the home, which made it seem they were being raised by a single mother. He learned that quality time and building a relationship were of no importance or value in a father, so in my lifetime I have only three fond memories of acts of love that my father and I shared.

Both my parents projected their unhealthy emotions and negative behavior onto my brother and me. It gave me a lack of self-love from not being affirmed and taught me to embrace rejection, to put myself last and make others a priority, to seek protection from any man who was willing to stay, and last that my life didn't matter. My parents' addictions were their first love, and ultimately both of their causes of death – my mother contracted HIV from her boyfriend who was an IV drug user, and my father had a heart attack caused by a drug overdose, deepening our affliction of abandonment as we found ourselves parentless. My father had already introduced me to abandonment when he and my mom ended their relationship, when my twin and I were in kindergarten. The abandonment of a father is intense for a son and a daughter. It taught my brother that it was okay to abandon my children and that seeing them was not a priority. It taught him that making wrong decisions was better than fighting to make good ones, and it also made him feel everyone had to make up for him being fatherless and motherless after their deaths. His sense of abandonment was solid and indefinite. But with the prayers my great-grandmother covered us with, he met his wife, and she had the patience of Job to deal with him and love him beyond everything he did that was grounds for her to abandon him. Ultimately, her love healed him and showed him commitment. For me, the abandonment of my father taught me that I was not of any value, I did not matter and men did not have to commit to me in a relationship to reap the benefits of one. It taught me unconsciously that I was not good enough to go on a date, to be courted, to have conversations with or to stay with. The absence of my father set the tone for all of my unhealthy relationships with men.

I was twenty-one years of age with two daughters when I got out of prison, and having no mother became the icing on the cake. The behavior I was raised in had become my influence to pass down to my daughters or to change to create generational blessings. We fight through life battling the pull from the behaviors of our parents, the strong holds passed down through generations, but the new morals we learn from others who were raised differently become a guiding light to discover a new road to a different outcome. The relationships we cultivate with people from a different dynamic or culture, the books we read and the movies we watch help us to develop a new narrative with new principles to create generational blessings with healthy behaviors. For me, everything finally changed when I began replacing the influence of my biological father with the influence of the ultimate Father. It was only when I began allowing Him to guide me and cover me that I was redeemed.

Psalm 27:10 (AMP): "Although my father and my mother have abandoned me, yet the Lord will take me up [adopt me as His child]."

REDEMPTION

Christianity was in my bloodline, even though I had not yet come to know God for myself. It has always been in the belief in hope and freedom for slaves and for my family. From my late Great-Great-Grandma Johnson to my Great Mama Sis and Grandma Mary, may they continue to rest in peace, my ancestors left me with the importance of covering your family in prayer and a relationship with God. And it continued with my Grama Snooky, who was an example of God's fruit, strength and unconditional love on earth. Their prayers and beliefs were familiar in my spirit yet unknown to my flesh.

Sharp Street United Methodist Church was my foundation as a child. When I began to seek different ways to heal the brokenness within as an adult, I found myself running from my addictive behaviors and the generational curses known to my family., I returned to the hope that seemed so safe and uplifting at First Mt. Olive Free Will Baptist Church, where the worship and spirit were comforting and emotionally moving, but I had not yet touched the surface of what a relationship with God would mean for me. When I sat in an evening service and heard a guest preacher from Greater Grace Harvest Church, his pure teaching of the Word of God sparked interest in me to learn more, and New Year's Eve 1999 was the beginning of me understanding salvation and learning how to live a life of Christ.

I had been a member of Greater Grace Church for eight years. Greater Grace was a place of commitment to my relationship with God, my sanctification and maturing from a babe in Christ. It was a solid foundation for who I am today. It was full of a body of believers my mother's and grandmother's age who had been in church all their lives, so I felt a level of disconnect or not belonging, but nonetheless I found spiritual parents whom I adored and would do anything to please. The relationships I cultivated within that ministry were life changing. I was in the company of some strong, virtuous women who loved, supported and nurtured their children in ways that were new to me.

I went through a sanctification process, maturing, tithing, building my faith, persevering through hardships and learning how to worship God and people. I had learned to sacrifice financially as I had invested in Catholic and Christian schools for both my daughters in elementary and high school, and my oldest had graduated from Grace Christian Preparatory Academy. I had purchased my first home, left for a year to live with my grandmother because I needed a new furnace and didn't have the money for one, and returned to my home, all during my tenure at Greater Grace. I was given a book called *The Shack* by one of my clients, and that book changed my life, my perspective and how I interpreted the Trinity. My mind shifted into a true relationship with God, and I began to dismantle my habits of pleasing people and the expectation of them filling the emptiness of not having parents. I had placed my spiritual parents in the space to replace my earthly parents, and I had been saying everything to keep from disappointing them, which led to my abandonment. So when the time came that I disagreed with them about not contributing support for Latia to participate in an honor program, it made me feel that I was not good enough for them to help me, and I tried a new tool to keep myself from being abandoned. I ran to protect myself.

In Matthew 18:12 it states, "If a man has a hundred sheep and one of them wanders away, what will he do? Won't he leave the ninety-nine others on the hills and go out to search for the one that is lost?" Well, I ran, but I wanted to be "the one" my spiritual father came after. Others in my church community did, but he did not, so though I ran and left the church, I could not escape the pain of abandonment. I yearned to be proven wrong and sought after like I was of value, but only one person could change my mind, my spiritual father, and it didn't happen. Our pain will have us putting expectations on people who don't have a clue and were never meant to. I was distraught because he was the first man who had ever wanted to be a father to me, who cared about me enough to show up, to tell me I was doing a great job in ministry and to love me like a daughter, even if it was spiritual. Greater Grace was my family, my support system. I had big sisters I aspired to be like spiritually, who covered me and prayed over me and my daughters. When I had to leave this family of relationships that had been the center of my life for eight years, I was broken. I had made them my parents, and the minute they disappointed me, the wounds of my childhood rejection burst open and bled again. The only protection I knew was myself, my familiar responses, and to run – and I did, far away from church. For good, I thought.

After being out of fellowship for months, I missed worship. There was more I needed to learn about my heavenly Father and myself, and if he had grown me to this level, surely I could grow beyond my brokenness. So I set out to find a new church home. I had visited the home churches of my clients and friends who would invite me, but God would not allow me to release the pain that sat in my chest. It was time for me to utilize the spiritual tools I had learned at Greater Grace, prayer and fasting, and I began to ask God to guide my steps. I fasted from Palm Sunday to Easter and ended up visiting what would become my new church home on Easter Sunday – New Zion Ministries, led by Pastor Clarence Jones and Angel Jones.

How? I went to the His Way Christian bookstore in Ellicott City to purchase reading material to help me grow spiritually during my fast. I ended up at the car dealer across the street, test driving an Acura MDX truck that I wanted. While I knew I was not making any major decisions until the end of my fast, I also knew what I could afford, and while I was waiting for financing, the car salesman began to tell me about his church and I realized it had never been about the car. I declined what they were offering and left. They called me up until Wednesday with alternative deals, but I turned them all down. I was obedient. God had done exactly what I asked – he had directed me to my new church home – and by my third Sunday visit I had come to know an unperfect church that I found to be a safe place for my daughters and myself. I finally cried out to God and released my pain at the altar!

New Zion Ministries showed me an unconditional love of God. It was women and men my own age and most were married couples. There were young ladies my daughters' ages. They were imperfect, and I felt okay to be myself. This was where I would come to know deliverance and healing from my past pain and begin a life of transformation, shedding guilt, pain and grief by seeking God and growing through the Word of God.

New Zion Ministries represented love, support and familiarity. It was the place where I saw my generation married and worshipping God imperfectly, and I wanted to share my life in marriage with a man of God. Still, when I started going to Bible study, I didn't realize I was the only woman most of the Tuesdays, until one week another woman did show up and her reaction towards me was unsettling. As I tried to figure out what her issue was, I realized here I was, a new beautiful woman at a new church in Bible study with all the husbands – I could see how she felt that way! God had blinded me because He knew I had a reverence for the sanctuary and His church. All I saw was an army of men to protect me as brothers in Christ, just as my uncles had protected me growing up, and that was exactly what happened. When I had a situation in camp concerning my daughters, they were supportive in helping me and sending me resources to address the situation.

I was enjoying my place of worship, learning more about the Kingdom of God and loving myself more than in my former years. It seemed like the only thing missing was a relationship. The safety I felt with the men around me in church could have been what the enemy used to awaken my addiction – and eventually he had his way. How did I come into a place in my life where I was enjoying a ministry that made me feel loved and protected, but also became the place where my old demons almost won me over and sucked me back into lustful bondage? I thought I had met my potential husband, a deacon of a church and an old interest who was about eight years older than me whom I had never had sex with because I was pregnant with my first daughter when he approached me. Here we were, twenty-two years later.

Shawn was my entanglement with the enemy. He looked like a godsend but was a trap of the enemy, and around him I welcomed spirits back into my life. I was at a place of letting go of my past battles with lust and embracing relationship God's way by abstaining from sex, but when I told him about my issue and that I wanted to turn a new leaf, he did everything in his power to awaken my flesh. He constantly talked about his previous encounters, of how and where he'd had sex, for example a fitting room in the middle of a store, and those conversations penetrated my ear gates and the lust of my flesh awakened. Before you knew it, I was enjoying the fulfillment of satisfying my body, and it was good. I couldn't get enough, and after creating another soul tie and having unprotected sex, I realized that he was a man who knew what women wanted and had no intention of being in a monogamous relationship. His lies caught up with him, but that didn't stop him. He just worked harder to lower me back into the saddle. It was a struggle to let him go, knowing he didn't want marriage, but I had physical fulfillment in all areas – foreplay, oral, penetration, size and all – for the first time in my life and that was very hard to let go! He would always say, "You're going to get what you want, be patient." One time I caught another female over at his house and stopped dealing with him for four months, but the minute I talked to him, he found a way to make it seem it wasn't what I assumed, and again logic went out the window. When you entertain demons, they come back with a vengeance.

He found a way to expose me deeper by inviting me into a threesome on my birthday weekend, and I obliged. Afterwards my intuition was confirmed and all of the answers I didn't have were right in front of me – I knew that she was also thinking she was in a relationship with him, and we both came face-to-face with reality. "Is that a gift to give someone you value on their birthday?" I asked myself, and I began to feel ashamed. The next day, while ushering at church, "How can you worship God after what you did last night?" was in my head, so I decided that was my last time in his bed. If I allowed my flesh to continue making decisions for me, surely I would die, and I had a reason to live, not just for me but for my daughters.

We still talked on the phone, but I declined his invitations to come over. I had been allowing lust to put me in a position where I could have gotten an STD, or worse, AIDS, and that spoke volumes to me that I didn't have enough strength to dance with the enemy and those demons and I needed God's help to cover me. I took my youngest daughter to a college tour in New York the following weekend with her dad and I realized he reminded me of Shawn with all his lies, and I asked myself, "Is this the example I want to set for my daughters?" So I finally had the willpower and two reasons to end my entanglement, and I chose myself and my future. I informed Shawn when I returned from New York that we were done. Of course he asked if we could be friends, and I declined. I had finally learned my addiction had to be cut off and never entertained again.

I was on a spiritual fast after Thanksgiving, seeking forgiveness from God and myself. I had a new mindset and was ready for a spiritual renewal in January after I signed up for a women's retreat. New Zion Ministries was the place I became authentically virtuous within myself. In my maturing, I stopped allowing my flesh to make decisions for me and embraced the spiritual transformation of becoming a Virtuous Woman. Saying "yes" to becoming a deacon was above all about me learning discipline and balance within my life, and being an example of Christ to my family and others. The process included four months of learning from God's Word what was expected of a deaconess, a sanctification process of sinning less and living righteously. It definitely didn't mean I became perfect, but I wanted to honor and please God more than my flesh, my emotions and my former addictions. I discovered principles that contribute to living a life pleasing to God, which all begin with the internal action of feeding the Spirit within and operating in the Fruit of the Spirit, which is love, joy, peace, patience, kindness, goodness, faithfulness, gentleness and self-control, along with serving my family. This was what I continued to focus on after my first leadership/diaconate class in church.

James 1:8: "A double-minded man is unstable in all his ways."

MY NAME CHANGE

The man who would become my husband and I had our first date four weeks after I closed the chapter of my entanglement.

I met Jamar Giddins through a Facebook group called SDIB (Speed Dating in Baltimore). One of the admins invited him and another invited me, but we had never gone to any of the speed dating events. Most of our interactions were within the group. Every day a person would post a question for the group, for example, if you have a degree, does the person of interest have to have one, and if so, what's the highest? Does it matter if the person of interest has natural hair or relaxed? If you are divorced, how long were you married, what did you learn from your prior marriage and are you willing to marry again? The questions sparked great conversations within the group, and we were able to get a feel for those responses that left an impression with us.

One day somebody posted a long message about love just being an emotion, and Jamar's response put him at the top of my interest list because it was a long biblical explanation of God's love which spoke to his relationship with God. Still, I didn't get too excited, because of my experience with the double-minded entanglement. After a month and a half of Facebook exchanges and meet-and-greet events, which we never made it to, Sandy the admin posted a scripture, Proverbs 18:22 – "He who finds a wife finds a good thing and obtains favor from the Lord" – and said, y'all have been hanging out and it's time to make some serious love connections. All the men had to send her a message naming the woman they were interested in dating with their email, and she would send them on to the woman's inbox, and it was up to her to respond. The first person whose email she sent me was someone who never really communicated in the group and I didn't even know he existed, and I also saw a picture of him smoking and that was a deal breaker for me, so I didn't respond – but my second email was from Jamar, and it said, "I'm very interested and would love to meet you." I responded, "The feeling is mutual."

Our first date was at TGIF. I was nervous. His profile picture looked nice, but he also looked familiar. He didn't have many pictures, though, so it seemed like a blind date to me. When he walked in, I realized I knew of him from when he was married to his former wife, whom I knew. We had all worshipped at Mt. Olive Freewill Baptist Church. It took me a minute to get over that, along with the fact that he was short. I realized about forty-five minutes into our conversation that I was enjoying him leading the dialogue, and I finally tapped into the date. It was December 30th, 2011, and he asked if we could see each other the next day. I said I would be worshipping for the New Year's Eve service and I was off to a women's retreat thereafter for three days, and since he worshipped at his own church the next day, we didn't have our second date until four days later.

After three months, we were really falling for one another, and our dating became a courtship, meaning we were both in a mindset for marriage and now dating with a purpose. We decided to start counseling to understand what marriage meant and if it was what we wanted. When December came, we celebrated our one-year anniversary and decided to transition into premarital counseling, and without a ring or a proposal, set a date to get married on July 7, 2013. Our relationship wasn't about jewelry, money or just being married. It was about love, God's approval and our commitment to understanding the covenant of marriage. On March 13, 2013, we hosted an engagement party for the wedding party, and Jamar surprised me and officially proposed with a ring. It wasn't the ring of a woman's dreams, but that didn't matter to me – the most important part was our marriage. Our decision to marry didn't go without negative whispers and conversation between family members and friends who didn't approve, but we learned to block out anything that did not promote celebration.

Pastor Jones and Angel Jones had counseled and prepared Jamar and me for marriage. It was an intense, challenging, life-changing process that sometimes extended for hours, and the Joneses were immensely powerful, effective and real in how they conducted our sessions. Counseling with them was a divine decision with the right couple who utilized God's principles of marriage and their experiences. We use those principles to get through challenges even now. The Church transitioned to a new location, and Jamar returned to his former church, where he missed serving on the media ministry. I was saddened that we were now worshipping in different places, but we came up with a plan that made me feel better.

Before we could put our plan into action, I went to Mentorship Miami, an intimate hair show that opened up the weekend with a Saturday evening worship service, and it was so powerful that God moved on my heart and delivered me from a violation of trust in my past that I didn't know I was still harboring. I realized I was missing worship that ushered in the presence of God, and I decided to follow my husband. The plan we had made never came to fruition, because my car went up and we were down to one vehicle. I felt like God was arranging things so we had to worship in one place. When Pastor Jones called to check on me because he felt my disconnect, he created a safe place for me to have honest conversation and he supported my transition to follow my husband. It was the turning point of a new experience with my spiritual fathers, and it brought me to tears. I knew it was hard for him to release me, but he knew that my life's purpose was greater than a church membership, and I will always respect and love him for his maturity in the matter. I may not have had a relationship with my biological father, but God has given me spiritual fathers to demonstrate the father relationship I never experienced.

As I matured in Christ and my husband found his "good thing," I began a new journey of life – God changed my name, as He commonly did in the Bible, with Abram, Jacob, Saul and Sarai, to signify new identity, life and purpose in God, leaving behind a life unpleasing or not of God. When my name changed to Giddins through marriage, I felt that I was given an opportunity of a new life, a new me who no longer has the generational curses that were attached to my maiden name. The girl you read about in the beginning of this book no longer existed.

There were relationships that could no longer proceed into my new identity, and they began to reveal themselves the moment I shared I was getting married. The two people I had come to love the most, my maid of honor and matron, did not have the capacity to love my new identity because they got too much out of mourning the broken me, so those relationships ended. I was grieved about losing them for some time until I got up and began to love the new opportunities that were in front of me.

One of the key relationships I had to let go of was both business and personal. The rift developed over a two-year time period that started with me giving back the partnership that had been given to me seven years prior. I remained as an employee, but there was a negative atmosphere, and the problems intensified until eventually I resigned. It began when I was excited to tell my friend that I was getting married and her response was not excitement or celebration but, "Well, we need to discuss protecting the salon's partnership from your marriage" I was hurt, but I was not going to allow that reaction to steal my joy, because there was no existing profit for me nor him to inherit. My partnership never afforded me anything other than what I worked hard for, my commission. I also found out six months after my wedding that she believed I had taken money from the company for my wedding. I was appalled, angry and hurt. In my seventeen years there, I had never taken, stolen or helped myself to any money, and I handled it every day. My paycheck for the week was more than what was in the bank, so I charged $736 on the business card instead of cashing my $1,200 check on Saturday, then woke up at seven a.m. the first day of my honeymoon to have the bank manager transfer $500 of the money back to the business account. I would pay the rest when I was able to cash my check. My old friend and business partner turned that entire situation around to make me out to be a thief, another reason our relationship was coming to an end.

We tried going to counseling to mend our business relationship, and I paid for two sessions of a therapist of her choice. But when she did not show up for a session, I realized this was a waste of my money and time. The therapist told me at the end that my partner had expressed that we could continue in separate sessions. When I left, I was so upset I called my husband and cried all the way home. The person I had pushed myself for all those years didn't show up for me and our relationship.

You would think that after all that I would be ready to quit, but I always found reasons to stay, like how much I loved all the clients, the other employees, anything other than myself, until the last straw. The salon and mentor whom I had come to love, and whose success I had spent seventeen years devoting my life to, had both come to an end because of an unprofessional exchange that happened between her and my daughter, who was an employee while the salon was full. There was an opportunity to recover the relationship, but she chose to stand by her actions. After helping my daughter pack up her station, I was angry for a while. I wanted to resort to my old behavior just to avenge the humiliation that my daughter had gone through, but I chose to fast and pray for God to direct me and release the anger. When I got confirmation that it was time to leave, I planned my exit from the business. I already knew I was dealing with an emotional person, so a two-week notice was not an option with her – and she definitely hadn't given my daughter that option when she told her to get out and leave. I finally had a conversation with her and resigned the same day.

I launched A Virtuous Touch Salon and Spa on Wednesday, April 29, 2015, after four weeks of planning. I did it afraid! I was starting over in my career, and I didn't know if I would lose a lot of clients whom I had built relationships with, but they followed me to the next phase, even though it was not what we were used to. I worked overtime to establish my new brand/baby.

God had transitioned my life three times within the first two years of my marriage, with friendships, a new business and a new church home. The evidence of my redemption in Christ and the investment of becoming a new creature on earth was being manifested, and yet poverty still showed itself within my old habits. I was tremendously uncomfortable in this newness of life.

I was a stranger in my new church, Dreamlife Worship Center, the president of a new corporation, a serial entrepreneur and moonlighting in another business, the Kolour Kulture. But despite my discomfort, these changes were the most impactful of my life, all preparing me for fully becoming who God had purposed me to be spiritually, in business and financially.

My life had changed because my circle had changed and my commitment was to myself and to my purpose, so my relationships and investments had to line up with who I was becoming. In those years I had taken two business classes with Empowering You Consulting in New York and a business leadership course with Dream Eagles Empowerment Network, invested in numerous classes and reacquainted myself with traveling for trade shows and with the Kolour Kulture. I was willing to invest time and money in where I was going, which exposed me to new opportunities. The spiritual leaders, mentors and friendships I now have understand who I am and celebrate me. God began to blow my mind once I allowed Him to direct my life. As I filtered through the days, months and seasons of the years following this paradigm shift, my mindset was renewed, and soon poverty became a memory in the rearview mirror.

I read a devotion that stated, "In a dream I kept going back to my childhood home only to find it vacated and desolate. Even though there is no going back, you can build on the foundation of things that made you strong." My life as Danielle Rogers no longer exists, but the pain of that life pushed me to become the woman I am today. I owe that to my relationship with Christ and my belief in the Trinity, and to all of those who played a part in my journey.

THE CHOSEN GENERATION

A generational curse is believed to be passed down from one generation to another due to rebellion against God or sinful habits or beliefs that negatively affect our lives or the lives of those around us. Our families have the greatest influence on our development, and the patterns of sin are passed down through them. Within my family we have a history of drug addiction, incarceration, teenage pregnancy, and abusive or dysfunctional relationships. I can trace these behaviors and patterns back five generations. Half of the thirteen children in the first generation pushed past them, and all three in the second generation, but the fourth generation were overtaken – four of them passed away, leaving only three, and two of those still battle with their demons on a regular basis.

I am part of the fifth generation, and we have come to understand that our lives are really about overcoming every obstacle, test, and painful situation that has come to steal our purpose. We have a belief in the Word of God and stand on the promises and strength of our heavenly Father and the prayers of our ancestors. We have a history of at least one sibling being overtaken. My cousin Antwon and I are the chosen of our fifth generation, and Kim C., Kim T., and Robin are the chosen of our fourth generation. We may have had some run-ins with the curses, but we persevered through to create generational blessings.

While our siblings had long battles with their drug addictions, they are now clean at the time of writing, except cousin Kirk, RIP. His sister built a career with the government and uses her gift of singing for the Lord within her church ministry. My cousin Kim T. graduated from high school after studying dance and moved to New York to pursue a career on Broadway, where she is now a creative makeup artist on movie and television sets. My cousin Kim C. graduated from an HBCU and now holds a VP position in human resources at her company. She also provides consulting as her own business and was the first to marry and remain in a loving, committed marriage of twenty years to a successful husband in banking. Antwon took a community approach, developing a marching band for the local children to give them an outlet. For two decades those children became his own. Shortly after he retired from that role, he began his own transportation company, and now he works in a hospital as a supervisor. They are all operating in freedom and enjoying life.

I am now living out my dream of owning my own salon, A Virtuous Touch Salon and Spa, where I am in partnership with my youngest daughter, Tykira Ceaser. I am the first to complete high school and trade school and to operate for twenty-three years as an entrepreneur in the beauty industry as a senior cosmetologist with my very own brick-and-mortar business. I was the first grandchild to purchase a home, eight years after prison, living outside the projects. I am the first grandchild to marry. I credit my success to my relationship with the heavenly Father as a believer and follower of Christ, and to the fact that I have learned forgiveness of those who didn't have the capacity to understand the pain they inflicted upon me or the capacity to love unconditionally. It's a never-ending cycle of "hurt people, hurt other people," and until we make a personal decision to seek healing and deliverance from the pain that was inflicted upon us, we will continue the cycle. I have learned that I have power to change the narrative and create blessings to leave upon and grow within the generations after me, as I work hard to leave a legacy for my children, their children and their children's children. I have learned to process through pain, because it has come to teach, prepare, and elevate me to another level of freedom in life. I have learned to accept a common principle: people come for a reason, a season, or a lifetime, and if they show you that the season is over, accept it and move forward. They don't have the capacity to experience what is coming next for you. People can't fill the holes and voids in your life; only God can deliver and heal you. Lastly, I have learned that although I am a powerful being in Christ, I don't have the ability to save, love or help others beyond themselves., I leave that to the ultimate savior Jesus Christ. As I ponder on the children of Israel, whose journey from Egypt to the Promised Land took forty years because of their mindsets still being entrapped in slavery, their disobedience, and their lack of ability to accept change rather than yearning for what was comfortable, I give thanks to God my freedom came in twenty years and not forty.

When I strategically changed my email address from chocolaterogers@hotmail.com to virtuousrogers@yahoo.com to virtuousgiddins@gmail.com, I was learning to accept the change within me throughout those years. The woman I had aspired to become, whom I had never seen fully realized in my life, was located in Proverbs 31, the virtuous woman. The last twenty-three years of my life were about becoming virtuous. As I prepare to sell my first home, where I raised my daughters, and embrace new beginnings, completing the sale will be the last time I sign my maiden name on legal documents. God has shown me the manifestation of his abundance during the COVID pandemic of 2020–2021. He has released a wealth transfer from the government for me to see the manifestation of my dream salon, and he has brought a cleaving process in my marriage after eight years to a place of one accord, love, and hope of a continued fulfillment with Jamar John Giddins. We have weathered a lot of storms in those years, but we fight together, and that's how we continue to have victory as we grow individually, spiritually, and as one in our marriage. One of those storms was my husband, grandson, and me all testing positive for COVID but having minimal symptoms, and I thank God that we accepted the blood of Christ to heal us, knowing it could have gone another way.

My four-year journey of writing this book is at its end. This process has given me deliverance from the things I pushed so far down that I forgot, acceptance and healing of my past so that it has no bearing on my future, and freedom to continue becoming who God has purposed me to be. The daughters I raised are now becoming even greater mothers than me and are operating in their areas of gifting. They have had the pleasure of blessing me with two amazing grandkids. They wined and dined me on Mother's Day at the ages of thirty and twenty-eight. The most amazing, significant, and ultimate ending to this book is that on May 2nd, 2021, a visiting pastor, Prophet Adelle, came to our church home, Dreamlife Worship Center, and spoke the Word of God over my life again, saying, "God said you are a virtuous woman, and what God is about to do in your husband's and your life concerning your marriage and your bloodline has not yet been seen." It left me in a state of awe that God would continue to speak to me, love me in public and affirm me even in my imperfection.

I have finally come to peace with the trials and tribulations that I have endured throughout my life. I can now embrace the self-love and value within myself, continue a path of freedom through my faith and believe in God's Word as I continue to become. I will always believe that "all things are possible with God if you believe."

This virtuous woman leaves you with this wisdom: It's not how you begin, it's how you end. Develop a mindset of embracing change, just like the seasons that we transition into four times a year. Remember that pain has the ability to transport you to your purpose if processed with forgiveness and seize the opportunity to learn from each decision, then move forward. Keep moving, don't become complacent in your life, and lastly, submit to a higher power and NEVER GIVE UP on YOU.

1 Peter 2:9: "But you are a chosen generation, a royal priesthood, a holy nation, His own special people, that you may

proclaim the praises of Him who called you out of darkness into His marvelous light."

"I am very proud of the completion of this book, which is a wonderful success story. I have witnessed my granddaughter at her worst and now have the pleasure of seeing the manifestation of every goal she set throughout her life."

Cecelia M. Jackson-Anderson

Made in the USA
Middletown, DE
09 October 2021